DIVINE PERSPECTIVES

A Bible Animal Story Collection

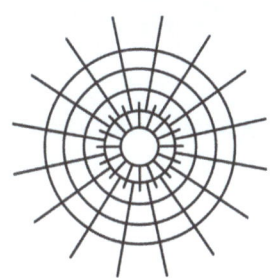

By Bruce McClain

Published 2024

Printed in the United States of America

First Edition
ISBN (softcover): 978-1-963380-02-6
ISBN (hardcover): 978-1-963380-03-3
ISBN (e-book): 978-1-963380-04-0

For information, address:
Holzer Books LLC
8 The Green, Ste. A
Dover, Delaware 19901 USA

For information about special discounts available for bulk purchases, sales promotions, and educational needs, contact:
info@holzerbooksllc.com
+1 (888) 901-7776

TO MY MOTHER, BETTIE MCCLAIN.

WITHOUT YOUR LOVE, GUIDANCE, AND SUPPORT,
THIS BOOK WOULD HAVE NEVER BEEN POSSIBLE.

INTRODUCTION

Divine Perspectives is a compilation of four short stories that takes you on a journey into the lives of four different and unique animals in the Bible. Their lives will show their courage, obedience and perseverance through personal struggles and trials. God continuously shows us His love in many ways and forms. God's love is forever present in our everyday lives and situations. As believers, we just need to listen for His voice and believe that we are all called according to His purpose.

PREFACE

I had never envisioned myself as a writer or even becoming the author of a book. While reading and studying the different stories in the bible, I would wonder why God chose to use the different animals in the ways that He did.

I felt that giving these animals a back story, would help bring an understanding to how God uses the ordinary, or the unlikely, to make the extraordinary happen.

These four stories took me over twenty years to complete. Not because of their complexities, but because of the personal events that were happening in my own life at the time. God always gave me bits and pieces when He saw fit to do so. I really feel that these stories were not written from my perspective; but from a divine perspective.

The Sacrifice

Once upon a time, when the earth was still young, there lived Alon, king of the wild sheep in the mountains of Moriah. Alon was a wise and beloved leader, strong in stature, with huge horns that were intimidating to even the strongest of challengers.

Alon loved his herd, but most of all he loved his wife, Hava. Hava was well respected among the other ewes or female sheep. Hava was very helpful when it came to helping the other sheep with their lambs. Although Alon and Hava desired children of their own, Hava's womb was barren. Sometimes, Hava would hear the other mothers laughing and making jokes about her, and this would hurt her deeply.

Alon being king, and by the laws of the herd, could mate with any of the other sheep, so that he could have male children to carry on his name.

Alon loved Hava so much that he wanted only her. Alon would console her under the warm star-filled night by saying, "Hava, my love, my love for you goes deeper than birthrights and deeper than laws. I talk to the Creator of us all, and he tells me that because of my faithfulness to him, he will be faithful to us, and that he will open up your womb, and I will have a son."

Hava looked at Alon in the eyes and said, "I am far past the age of childbearing. Maybe you should start looking at some of the younger ewes."

Alon raised up on both hind legs, lifted his horns high in the air, and when he came down on all four legs, he lunged forward slamming his horns into a large boulder.

Two years have passed, and every day during that time, Alon would speak the prophecy that the Creator gave to him into Hava's life.

One morning, just as the sun started to crest over the horizon, the Creator came and spoke to Alon and Hava.

"I am that I am. I am the Alpha and the Omega, the beginning and the end. All that your eyes can see was created because I spoke it into existence. Hava, if by my word all was created, then my word should cause your womb to obey."

"Oh! Forgive me for my unbelief," cried out Hava.

"Alon and Hava, when I created you, I did so with purpose. The names that you possess were given to you with a specific intention in mind. Hava, your name means life-giving; for soon you will give birth to a son. Alon, your name means *oak tree*, for one day you are going to have to stand strong and deep-rooted in faith and love for me."

"Alon and Hava, this very spot in which you are standing will one day be a proving ground for one man's faith. A man whom I love dearly, a man with whom I have a covenant, a man to whom I also promised a son."

Soon after Alon and Hava's meeting with God, Hava conceived, and five months later, gave birth to a son, just as God had promised. Alon was very proud, and he blessed

and thanked God for keeping His promise. That night, an angel of the lord appeared to Alon and instructed him to name his son Asher, which means *blessed*.

Asher grew to be strong, wise, and handsome. Alon was very protective of his son, and as the years passed, Asher developed beautiful horns, but never as big as his father's.

"Father," Asher said, "will I be king one day just as you are?"

Alon looked at his son with admiration and said, "Yes, you will, but you must become stronger first because you will always be challenged by those seeking to take that which you rightfully inherited."

One day in the early months of spring, when Asher was nearly an adult, he and some other males were playing in the northern part of Mount Moriah. Asher's horns became entangled in a thorn bush, and the harder he tried to escape, the more trapped he became. Asher yelled to his friends to go and get his father. Asher knew that many sheep and rams had lost their lives to predators after becoming stuck in thorn bushes. He was very afraid.

"Do not be afraid, Asher, for I am with you. I am He who created everything, and there is nothing that is created that I did not create," reassured the voice.

Asher said, "My father told me about you many times and how I should trust in you and have faith in you."

The voice continued, "Asher, do you trust and believe in me?"

"Yes," Asher said.

"Then know that I will never leave you nor forsake you, for everyone and everything is born with a purpose."

The young rams reached Alon and explained to him what had happened. Alon's heart dropped, and without a word, he ran for the northern part of Mount Moriah. When Alon arrived, he stopped and looked down. In the lower valley, Alon saw an elderly man, and the elderly man was with a boy. Alon was confused because the man placed the boy on the wooden table that they had built and lifted a large knife up as if to kill the boy. Suddenly, the man looked up as though someone was speaking to him. He put the knife down and looked behind him.

In a thorn bush behind the man was Asher, but he was not thrashing and kicking, trying to escape; he was calm but scared. The man, seeing Asher in the bush turned back towards the boy, grabbed him, embraced him, and then threw his hands in the air, shouting into the sky.

At that time, there was a bright light in front of Alon, and the voice of God spoke to him. "Alon, I am the God of the man that you saw in the valley. His name is Abraham and his son, is Isaac. This is the man that I spoke to you about years ago. Remember when I told you what your name meant and how one day you would have to stand strong with faith and love for me?"

"Yes," Alon replied.

"Well, this is that time. Abraham needed to prove his faithfulness to me by the willingness to sacrifice his only son. As you saw, Alon, he was willing to offer his son back to me. Alon, are you willing to do the same?"

"But that is my legacy stuck in the bush," Alon replied.

"Yes," God replied, "and your legacy will pave the way for my son on this very spot." And on that day, on that hill, Abraham named that place *Jehova-jira - God will provide*.

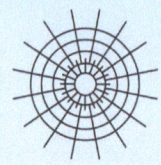

The Lion's Den

Once upon a time in the land of kings lived a pride of lions. These magnificent creatures ruled the prairies of Africa with honor and grace. This story is about one particular male lion that is only about ten months old. His father named him Bakari when he was born, just days before his death by African hunters. The name Bakari means *promising*, for his father hoped that one day his son would grow to be strong and wise and lead the pride just as his father and grandfather had, to fulfill everything he was unable to.

It was early February on the savanna, two months before Bakari would have to go through a rite of passage. This was a test of bravery and courage that would be given to the males around their first birthday.

"Mother," Bakari said, "what was my father like? Was he brave? Was he strong?"

"Bakari," his mother replied, "your father was both strong and brave, he was also very handsome. You remind me of him every time I look at you."

"If he was so strong and so brave," said Bakari, "then why was he not the head of the pride like my grandfather?"

His mother answered him, "Bakari, sometimes being strong and brave is not enough to be the leader of a pride. When your father was a young lion and had gone through his rite of passage about two years prior, this was a time of drought, and the pride had to travel far away to find water. One night, human hunters came and captured several of our males and females. Your father tried to fight the hunters and was injured by a poisoned arrow. He managed to escape and make it back to where the remainder of the pride had gathered. Your father became very sick from the poison and nearly died. He soon recovered, but his heart remained weak."

She continued, "Your father knew that he could never challenge any of the other young lions; for fear that his heart would fail him. Because of this, he would never be able to continue the legacy of his family that had been for many generations. Your father knew that one day he would have a son, and that son would grow and continue the legacy of his family."

"Mother, are you crying?" Bakari said. "Why are you so sad?"

"Yes, these are tears you see, but I am not sad. These are tears of joy because I am so blessed to have my only child be a male. I loved your father very much, and I miss him too."

The rite of passage for a young male lion consisted of several different tests. It starts with a two-day survival test that consists of navigating through hills, jungle, and desert terrain. The day test will end at the challenge grounds, a location where a series of skill challenges will take place, ending with the rite of passage ceremony. Young male lions from several different prides will participate in the passage tests.

One day, while Bakari was practicing for the tests, he heard a strange noise on the other side of a group of bushes. These were very strange sounds that he had never heard before. Bakari's curiosity got the best of him, so he walked into the bushes and peeked through. What Bakari saw nearly took his breath away.

The leader of the pride is an older, proud, and arrogant lion of around twenty years old who went by the name of Adika. After the death of Bakari's grandfather, the leadership of the pride was given to the father of Adika. It was given to him because none of the other lions were brave enough to challenge him for the position. When Adika's father became too old to lead the pride, Adika was there to take on his rightful inheritance, but unlike his father, he had four challengers who wanted the right to lead the pride just as bad as Adika. The challengers stood no chance against the strength and quickness of Adika, so the pride was his for the taking.

Adika had twin sons who would be going through the rite of passage ceremony along with Bakari.

On the other side of the bushes, Bakari saw some women from a nomadic tribe gathering water from the spring. The women were laughing while filling their jars with water. The sound of the women was strange to Bakari because this was the first time that he had come into contact with humans. Bakari heard a voice from behind him say, "be very quiet and back up slowly" - it was his mother!

"Bakari, do you know what you were doing?"

"Mother, where did you come from?"

"That's not important, Bakari; the important thing is that you realize the importance of what just happened."

"I don't understand, mother; those humans, they did not seem so dangerous, they were frail and fragile; I could have broken them in two with one bite."

"Yes, those humans that you saw were weak, that is because they were the female species of humans. The humans that you have to worry about are the males, the hunters, the killers. Bakari, promise me that in the future, if you ever come in contact with humans, you will run in the opposite direction."

"Yes, mother, I promise."

"I love you, Bakari."

"I love you too, mother."

It was a cool, clear night and all the stars were visible. "Just think, Bakari," his mother said, "tomorrow you will be a functioning member of the pride after your rite of passage ceremony. This will be the beginning of a wonderful life for you."

"I am so excited," said Bakari. "I will make you proud tomorrow, mother."

"I know you will, Bakari. Now go to sleep so that you will be well-rested."

The next day, lions from all around came out to the challenge grounds. This was an exciting day for all. Bakari and his mother arrived early. Soon the opening ceremonies began; it started with a large procession led by all of the pride leaders; Adika really stood out from the other pride leaders - maybe it was because of his arrogance; he just appeared larger than the others.

Following the pride leaders came all of the young lions participating in the ceremony. There were around fifteen young lions, and in the middle of them walked Bakari. Following the young lions came the elders, both male and female, and following the elders came all of the young lionesses from all of the prides. The young lionesses represented the future fertility of the prides.

The overseer of the rite of passage ceremony was an elderly lion who is still the leader of his pride. With confidence and grace, he stood before the multitude and gave out the instructions and procedures to the young lions. The air was thick with anticipation. At the end of the speech, the elderly lion let out a huge roar, and the young lions were off.

Two miles into the challenge, Bakari and four other lions fell into a deep pit. "Are you guys okay?" Bakari asked. One of the other lions asked if this was a part of the ceremony, and Bakari responded, "No, I think this is a trap set by human hunters."

"Quiet," said one of the lions. "I hear something coming."

The lions looked up and saw humans standing around the opening to the hole. One of the humans raised his arm, and the other humans lifted up blow darts to their mouths and shot darts into the hole. In no time at all, the lions were fast asleep.

An angel of the Lord visited Bakari in the form of a dream and said, "The one who created you and everything that is, sent me to tell you, that He is with you, and it was He that has caused you to be captured. The Creator of all needs to use you in a special way. You and the other lions captured, will be taken to a land far away, a land where the people there have captured the chosen people of the Creator. When you arrive in this land called Babylon, you will be placed into a pit, you will be denied food for several days, causing you to be very hungry. The king of Babylon will be forced to throw one of the Creator's chosen people into the pit in which you are kept captive, with the expectation of him being devoured. I was sent to convince you, and to convince the other lions, to restrain from consuming the man that is thrown into your den. The Creator has promised to deliver you out of the hands of your captives, in exchange for your obedience."

Bakari waited until they arrived in Babylon and placed in the pit to inform the other lions of the angelic visitation that he had while asleep. It took a while before the young lions agreed to restrain from attacking the human whenever he was thrown into the pit. The lions were in the pit for five days without any food. Tempers were rising, and Bakari constantly had to reassure them that they would be rewarded for their obedience.

One evening, a large group of men approached the opening to den and tossed a man into the pit. The lions jumped to their feet, including Bakari. The man huddled himself in a corner of the den. Bakari looked at the man and noticed a strange glow surrounding him. Despite their hunger, the lions restrained. In the morning, Bakari and the other lions were awakened by someone at the top of the den rejoicing; it was the king of Babylon. The king ordered his men to remove the man from the pit, and because the king felt that God had his hand on the lions, he ordered that the lions be removed from the pit, given a distinctive marking, and returned to the location of their capture. The king made a decree, that no lion bearing the markings of the king should be harmed.

When Bakari and the other lions returned to their homeland, a period of six months had gone by since their captivity. The lions' return home ignited joy and happiness among the prides all across the land. Bakari became a hero among the lions, and when Adika became too old and weak to lead the pride, Bakari stepped in to compete for the

position. But out of respect for Bakari, no other challengers came forth. Bakari's mother was very proud of her son, and he led the pride well, for many years.

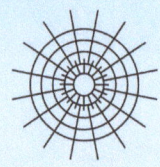

The Colt and The King

Once upon a time, in a town called Bethlehem, on a little farm just on the edge of town, lived a donkey by the name of Chavvah. In Hebrew, Chavvah means *life*; this was a name given to her by her owner who knew that she was special. Chavvah's mother was a hard-working donkey and was loved by the owners twelve-year-old daughter, Nissa. Nissa's father named the donkey Reena, which means *joy* because she bought so much joy to his daughter. When Reena had finished all of her work for the day, which consisted of carrying water, and firewood to the farm, and goods to be sold at the marketplace, Nissa would go out to the barn, put feed in Reena's manger, and brush her back. Reena looked forward to this special treatment every day.

"You think that you are so special," said Ufara, an older cow that lived in the stall next to Reena. "You are no better than the rest of us. I produce more milk than any cow in Bethlehem, but you carry the milk that I produce to market, and you get all the credit."

"I am not looking for credit, or favor, Ufara. I am just doing what I am supposed to do. Everyone knows how much milk you give, and I am sure that you are worth more than I am. I am expendable, but you are invaluable. I can be replaced with any other donkey, but no other cow can replace you."

"I never thought of it like that," said Ufara as she put her head back in her manger and grabbed a mouth full of hay.

On a nearby farm lived a strong and handsome male donkey by the name of Amasay, which means *burdensome*. Nissa's father and the owner of Amasay made a deal to mate the two donkeys. After the harvest, Reena was taken to the pasture of Amasay.

"What is your name?" asked Amasay.

"My name is Reena. And what is your name?" Reena asked.

"I am called Amasay," he replied. "You have a beautiful name, Reena.",

Reena paused and replied shyly, "Are you the only donkey on this farm?"

"No, there are ten female donkeys, but I am the only male. I have five sons and four daughters by those females, but I can tell you right now, that your beauty, I have never seen before.

Blushingly, Reena said, "Thank you."

Reena stayed with Amasay for one month and then was returned to her farm. When Reena returned back to the farm, Nissa ran out to the barn, hugged Reena, and brushed her with loving strokes. Reena was glad to be back home.

Reena continued to work for a while, but soon she was replaced by a younger donkey. Nissa would come and get Reena in the morning and take her to the pasture where she would just eat all day long. She did not know why she was so hungry all the time. Reena also could feel that she was gaining weight.

"You said that you could be replaced, and you were right," said Ufara. "And you are gaining so much weight. You are becoming as fat as a cow," she added while laughing at her own joke. "Oh, my goodness, I just realized, you are going to have a colt. It all makes sense," exclaimed Ufara. "You are going to be a mother!"

In the months to follow, Reena and Ufara became close friends. Ufara made sure that Reena had everything that she needed. Finally, the time had come for Reena to give birth.

Everyone was there in the barn, including the farmer's daughter Nissa. There was a lot of commotion going on. Ufara tried hard to stretch her neck so that she could see what was going on. All of a sudden, Nissa came running out of Reena's stall, screaming and crying. Soon, Ufara saw why the little girl was so upset. During the delivery, Reena had died because her colt was breached inside of her.

For days, there was a strange quietness on the farm. The farmer would come into the barn and bring the young colt into Ufara's stall and let her nurse the young donkey. This went on for about one week, and then the young colt was sold to an innkeeper in town because the farmer's daughter did not want the colt around. She blamed her for the death of her favorite pet, Reena.

The inn was located in the heart of Bethlehem. The city of Bethlehem sits on a limestone ridge about 2500 feet above sea level in the country of Judah. The town is about five miles south of Jerusalem, surrounded by fertile fields, vineyards, and olive orchards.

The innkeeper named the colt Chavvah. Chavvah worked hard year after year, carrying firewood, pulling carts, and plowing fields. Chavvah was made fun of and ridiculed by the other animals because her womb was closed.

The town of Bethlehem started to fill with visitors from all parts of the country. They were in Bethlehem because Caesar Augustus, the emperor of Rome, decreed that a census should be taken throughout the nation. Everyone was required to return to their ancestral home for registration.

The innkeeper was very excited, for this was an opportunity of a lifetime for him. The innkeeper worked Chavvah extra hard, almost to the point of being cruel. One night, Chavvah was awakened by a lot of noise in the barn. Chavvah arose and looked over the door to her stall; she saw a man and a woman come into the barn. The woman was riding on the back of a donkey, and she was with child. Chavvah could see everything going on as though it was daytime, for the starlight was bright that night, as though it was shining directly into the barn.

The innkeeper placed the donkey that the woman was riding, in the same stall as Chavvah. "What is all the commotion about?" asked Chavvah.

"Oh! This is a special night," said the donkey. "You are so lucky to be able to witness what is about to happen."

Suddenly, the innkeeper came over to Chavvah's stall and yelled back to the couple, "We can use this manger to lay the child in when he is born."

Chavvah said, "They are going to have the baby now?"

"Not just any baby," said the donkey, "this child is going to be the king of the Jews!"

This was very puzzling to Chavvah because she could not understand why a king would be born in a dirty stable. "Why did they choose to give birth here?" said Chavvah.

"No, it was not their choice; there was no room in the inn, every room in the town is occupied," explained the donkey.

Soon there was a glow coming from the area in the barn where the couple was. Chavvah looked over the door of her stall and saw a little baby lying in her manger. She knew at that moment, that this was a special child. Soon, men came to visit the child and laid gifts at the foot of the manger.

Soon, the young family had left the barn, but there was a peaceful spirit left behind. Something was different in the atmosphere; it was something that Chavvah had never felt before.

The morning after the family had left, the innkeeper came into the barn and returned the manger to Chavvah's stall. He was singing and whistling; Chavvah wondered if it was because he had made so much money, or if he felt the same spirit left behind by the family.

Chavvah noticed that eating from the manger was different; the hay seemed to taste better, not that it wasn't good before. While working she seemed to have more energy. She would hardly be tired at the end of the day. The innkeeper started treating Chavvah better because her productivity had picked up two hundred percent. There was something special about that manger, and Chavvah knew what it was.

Thirty-three years had passed since that wonderful night in the barn, but it was just like yesterday in the mind of Chavvah. One morning, Chavvah became very sick and could not get up. The innkeeper was very worried, for this was the day that he went to the marketplace to pick up his supplies for the week. He called in a doctor to look at her. When the doctor arrived, he poked and prodded, he poked and he pulled; then he stepped back, smiled, and said, "She is going to have a colt." The innkeeper's mouth fell open; he turned pale and then he leaped for joy, shouting, "It's a miracle, God had blessed her womb, for she is forty years old, well past her childbearing years."

People heard of the miracle and would stop by the barn to see Chavvah. The innkeeper would tie her to the front post of the inn so that people could see her. Chavvah brought in a lot of new customers for the inn keeper. Soon, Chavvah gave birth to her colt, and she named her Chenya, which means *grace of the Lord*.

The inn keeper continued to exploit Chavvah and her colt by tying them outside of the inn to attract new customers. One afternoon, two men walked up to Chavvah and the colt. They were very kind men, for their spirit was not as ordinary men. The men untied the colt, and the inn keeper came running out of the door, yelling, "Stop thief, why are you stealing my colt?" One of the men said, "We are not stealing the colt; we are disciples of the Lord Jesus Christ, and he sent us here to get the colt."

The innkeeper, along with all of the other citizens of Bethlehem, had heard about Jesus and was expecting his arrival. The innkeeper agreed to let the two men take the colt, they also took Chavvah with them. When they had arrived to where Jesus was, Chavvah knew that this was the same child that lay in his manger that wonderful night. Jesus walked over to Chavvah, placed his hand on her forehead, and looked into her eyes as though he had known her. The disciples placed their clothes on Chavvah and her colt. Jesus mounted the colt and they began to walk back towards Bethlehem.

A great multitude of people lined the streets, cheering and shouting. As Jesus passed, they laid down their clothes, and some people laid down branches from palm trees on

the ground, and others followed them into Bethlehem, crying, "Hosanna: Blessed is he that cometh in the name of the Lord" (Mark 11:9).

As Chavvah walked, she marveled at how happy and joyful the people were. She began to look deeply into the crowd, and as she looked, her eyes paused and fixed on a little girl holding a rooster.

"What a strange sight," Chavvah thought; suddenly her eyes were staring into the eyes of the rooster, and for a split second, she felt a strange kinship with the bird. Chavvah quickly turned her head back to concentrate on her colt and the Man she was carrying.

Chavvah was never so proud in all her life. She saw everyone that she knew, even the innkeeper.

After that day, Chavvah never had to work again. She spent the remainder of her life in green pastures and drank from still waters.

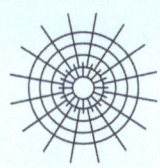

A Rooster in The Garden

The sun began to rise over the horizon in the east. The gates to the city of Jerusalem were still closed. Soon, they will open, and the city would come to life. Merchants would unlock their shops, and the enticing smells of the market place would waft Jerusalem.

There was a distinct buzz in the air. People seemed unusually excited; individuals who would typically be rude and unemotional were now smiling and greeting everyone who passed by. There was certainly something peculiar the atmosphere.

"Papa, can I go to the city gate? Everyone will be there." Remiel looked at his daughter with a look of unbelief because he knew precisely why she wanted to go. "Papa, the man named Jesus, the one who has been performing all the miracles and teaching in the synagogues, is arriving. Everyone is saying that he is the Messiah."

"Aliza, my beautiful daughter, I do not think that it would be wise for a ten-year-old girl to venture to such an event with so many people, all alone."

"I won't be alone," explained Aliza, "Eran will be with me." This visibly angered her father because Eran was a rooster, and not just an ordinary rooster; you see; Eran was born without a voice. Eran had never made a noise since birth, while all the other roosters his age have been crowing for a long time now.

As a young rooster, it is very important to be able to crow as soon as possible; this is the only way to get respect from the older roosters and young hens. The inability to make a single sound would result in a lack of respect, and instead, one would be looked down upon.

Aliza continued to plead with her father; but to no avail. Aliza ran from the house, angry that her father would not even listen to what she had to say about the man from Nazareth named Jesus.

Eran looked confused as Aliza ran by him; immediately, he ran after her. Aliza ran all the way up to the garden not far from their house. The garden was very beautiful and peaceful, full of olive trees and beautiful flowers. Aliza and Eran would always come to the garden and sit for hours, enjoying each other's company.

The roosters of Jerusalem were very proud. The took pride in the fact that the citizens of Jerusalem depended on them to signal when it was time to rise in the morning and when it was time to go to bed in the evening. Not being able to crow sometimes made Eran feel sad, is if he lacked a purpose. However, upon seeing Aliza in the morning, those feelings quickly disappeared.

When Eran caught up to Aliza in the garden, he found her pacing in circles underneath a large olive tree. She appeared very upset about something.

"Eran," Aliza said, "I can't believe my father would not even listen to me. If he knew more about Jesus, he would let me go, or he would even want to go himself. Eran, we need to go and see who this Jesus is. I want to see perform some miracles; maybe he will raise some dead people from the grave. Perhaps he could even give you a voice to crow. Wouldn't you like that, Eran? Now, do you see why we must go to the city gates?"

When Aliza and Eran returned home after visiting the garden, her father ran out to meet them. With joy and excitement in his voice, Remiel said, "Hurry, Aliza! You were right. We must go to the city's gate to welcome this Jesus. Everyone has been talking about this man and the wonderful miracles he has done."

"Is he a king?" Aliza asked her father. "Some people say that he is, and some say that he is the Messiah that we all have been waiting for. Father, who do you say that he is?"

"I don't know, Aliza," her father replied. "I really don't know."

When they arrived at the gate, a crowd had already started to gather. Aliza, Eran and her father luckily found a spot up front.

"Aliza, you have to hold Eran in your arms," her father explained.

"Okay," Aliza replied. "Wow, Eran, you are getting heavy," Eran welcomed being held because he was very tired from the long walk they had just made.

Suddenly, there was a great roar of cheers. People were yelling "Hosanna" and "blessed is he that cometh in the name of the Lord." Soon the procession was passing by them, and Eran looked on in amazement. Eran wished that he could have let out a loud crow to honor the man on the donkey, but all he could do was watch. As Eran looked, he noticed a donkey walking with the colt that was carrying Jesus. "That must be the colt's mother," and just as he thought that, the donkey looked over at him, and their eyes met, and the donkey smiled at him.

The procession passed, and some people followed, but Aliza's father said, "Let's go, Aliza, for we have many chores to do," and they left for home.

The days following the triumphant entry into the city by Jesus seemed to be getting a little strange. The joyful chatter that once filled the air, turned into bitter language and gossip. It seemed as though the same people who proclaimed their love for Jesus were now turning against him and his disciples.

One evening, while Aliza and Eran were playing in the garden, they heard voices and arguing. Aliza ran over to see what all the noise was about. A crowd had gathered in the garden. There were also Roman soldiers, and in the middle of the crowd was Jesus and his disciples. One of the disciples drew his sword and swung it at the servant of the high priest. Aliza saw the right ear of that servant fall to the ground. Jesus, without saying a word, bent down, picked up the ear, and placed it against the servant's head. When Jesus removed his hand, the ear of the servant was completely healed. The Roman soldiers grabbed Jesus and took him away. Aliza looked in amazement, for in the middle of the angry crowd was her father.

Aliza grabbed Eran and ran after the crowd. She had noticed that all of the disciples who were with Jesus had left, all except one. He was the one that cut off the ear of the servant, she thought.

Soon, the crowd stopped in the middle of a courtyard, and the disciple sat down with them. Aliza walked up to the disciple, looked at him closely, and said, "This man was with Jesus."

The disciple looked at Aliza and denied it, saying, "Woman, I don't know him."

A little later, someone else saw him and said, "You are also one of them."

"Man, I am not!" the disciple replied.

Aliza and Eran continued to follow the crowd. Eran was so confused; he could not understand why the crowd that loved Jesus a week ago could turn on him and be so mean. He could not understand why the disciple that tried to protect Jesus an hour ago now denied knowing him. Anger started to build up in the heart of Eran.

Just then, a man said, "Certainly, this fellow was with him, for he is a Galilean."

The disciple replied, "Man, I don't know what you are talking about."

Eran looked to his right and saw Jesus looking straight at him. Eran felt a surge of electricity surge throughout his whole body. His beak opened wide, and the loudest crow anyone had ever heard came flowing out of his mouth. At that moment, at that time, Jesus took the time to heal a little rooster and give him an important voice that would be recorded in history for all time.

Afterword

I had never envisioned myself as a writer or even becoming the author of a book. While reading and studying the different stories in the Bible, I would wonder why God chose to use the different animals in the ways that He did.

I felt that giving these animals a back story, would help bring an understanding to how God uses the ordinary, or the unlikely, to make the extraordinary happen.

These four stories took me over 20 years to complete. Not because of their complexities, but because of the personal events that were happening in my own life at the time. God always gave me bits and pieces when He saw fit to do so. I really feel that these stories were not written from my perspective; but from a divine perspective.

Acknowledgements

I would like to take this time to acknowledge the people in my life who have encouraged and supported me to become the person that I am today. Thank you, mom, for grafting in me that God should always come first. My siblings, Tonga, Victor, Fred, and Diane, thank you for always giving me your love and support. Thank you to my two children, Genesee and Bruce Jr., whom I love very much. Your support means the world to me. To Koda, the mother of my children, thank you for always making sure that we stayed rooted and grounded in the word of God. A special thank you to Diana Pullins; you always encourage me to be better, and strive for the impossible. Thank you, everyone, for making this book possible. I love you all.

www.ingramcontent.com/pod-product-compliance
Lightning Source LLC
Chambersburg PA
CBHW041434120626
46547CB00002B/207